The Language of Bones
American Journeys Through Bardic Verse

The Language of Bones
American Journeys Through Bardic Verse

Poems by

Elizabeth Spencer Spragins

Kelsay Books

Copyright 2019 Elizabeth Spencer Spragins. All rights reserved.
This material may not be reproduced in any form,
published, reprinted, recorded, performed, broadcast, rewritten
or redistributed without the explicit permission of
Elizabeth Spencer Spragins.
All such actions are strictly prohibited by law.

Cover design: Shay Culligan

ISBN: 978-1-949229-98-1

Kelsay Books Inc.

kelsaybooks.com
502 S 1040 E, A119
American Fork, Utah 84003

Contents

Jane	7
Trail of Tears	8
Chatham Manor	10
Traveller	12
Angels of Marye's Heights	13
Holy Grail	14
Restitution	16
The Tryst	18
Thunder Lizards	20
Grace	21
Longing	22
The Weather Vane	23
The Cherokee Wedding	24
Once	26
After the Day	28
Border Walls	30
Polar Night	31
Hunters	32
Northern Lights	34
At Standing Rock	36
Gemstones of the Desert	38
Sedona	39
The Garden of the Gods	40
Sacred Songs	42
Spires	45

Afterword
Notes
Acknowledgments
About the Author

Jane

(A *Cywydd Llosgyrnog*)

The hunger pads on restless paws
And probes the palisade for flaws.
Jaws devour the gate barred thrice—

Then hunger hews my flesh from bone
And gnaws my name from graveless stone,
Hones the blade of sacrifice

That hovers over every head.
We dine on horror, drink our dread,
Bury dead in snow and ice.

My eyes are lifeless, yet I laid
The table as my mistress bade.
Debts are paid, a meal my price,

But guests I fed will never dare
To meet my disembodied stare—
Fasting prayer can nourish vice.

The dark without, the dark within,
The deadly fangs of moccasin
Taint the linn[1] of paradise.

~The Voorhees Archaearium, Jamestown, Virginia

---

[1] A pool beneath a waterfall

Trail of Tears

(A *Rannaigheacht Ghairid*)

Fairy stones
Mark the graveless broken bones
Deep beneath the Trail of Tears.
Splintered spears and ghosts of crones

Cannot hold
Ancestral lands veined with gold.
Driven west through snow and mire,
People of the Fire grow cold.

Lullabies
Cannot soothe the hungry cries
Of babes in the arms of death—
One last breath breaks earthly ties.

Spirits roam,
Searching for blue hills of home.
Keepers of the sacred flame
Cannot tame the dark at gloam.[2]

---

[2] Twilight

Priest intones
Prayers for wounded earth that groans.
In dark shafts no gold appears—
Crystal tears yield fairy stones.

~Fairy Stone State Park, Stuart, Virginia

Chatham Manor

(A *Rhupunt*)

On this high hill
Young soldiers mill
About until
Dusk snuffs the light.

Though smoke and haze
Obscure their gaze,
They spot a blaze
That licks the blight

From rebel shire.
St. George's spire
Evaded fire—
The shots veered right

But pummeled walls
Of homes and halls.
Now cannonballs
Besiege the site.

The wounded moan
While brothers hone
Their hate on bone
And blood and fright.

The cruel kiss
Of demon's bliss
Has fathered this
Uncivil fight.

~Chatham Manor, Fredericksburg, Virginia

Traveller

(A *Rannaigheacht Ghairid*)

Coat of gray—
Curry combed and boxed away
With memories that faded.
Shaded shadows on the bay

Cup the cold:
Faces from the past, charcoaled
Onto hollows of the heart,
Start to blur as years unfold.

Hoof beats pound—
Spectral mount flies over ground,
Pursues the days that war claimed
When soldiers tamed Hell's bloodhound.

No more fray.
Horse and rider rest today,
Yet the weight of duty's sheath
Lies beneath a coat of gray.

~Lee Chapel Museum, Washington and Lee University,
   Lexington, Virginia

Angels of Marye's Heights

(A *Rhupunt*)

On cold, clear nights
The sacred sites
Of Marye's Heights
Turn back the year.

Shells blaze and burst,
Butcher the cursed.
Torment with thirst
Is Hell's hot spear.

Over the rise
Drift moans and cries,
And hopeless eyes
Plead pain and fear.

Then angels tread
The field of red.
Water and bread
Of life appear.

From hate's deep wells
Soft music swells—
The Sanctus bells
I cannot hear.

~Fredericksburg, Virginia

Holy Grail

(A *Clogyrnach*)

The statue of Saint Francis stands
With placid smile and quiet hands
Beneath a scarred birch
Where supplicants perch—
A quaint church
On torn lands.

Thick ivy clings to graves and grows
Untended over stones in rows.
A blanket of moss
Has softened love's loss—
On each cross,
Weathered prose.

A furtive form, a runaway,
Collapses, wounded, on the clay
Where merciful dead
Lie restless in bed.
Weak with dread,
Gnarled hands pray.

He pants despite the twilight's chill,
Then hears above the whippoorwill
A heart-stopping sound:
The bay of a hound.
Face to ground,
He lies still.

A rabbit at the statue's base
Takes flight downhill; the dogs give chase.
A lone overseer
Rides hard at the rear,
Passes near,
Sees no trace.

The hunted flees his hiding place
For Rappahannock's swift embrace.
Once captive, now free,
He mulls mystery—
On bent knee
Whispers grace.

~Fredericksburg, Virginia

Restitution

(A *Clogyrnach*)

A lone horse plods down William Street,
The carriage filled but for one seat.
As steel rings on stone,
The weary springs groan.
Insects drone
In June's heat.

No others wander Market Square.
The driver whistles to the mare.
The coach draws near; he
Reins in; one hand free
Motions me
To the stair.

I mount the carriage in a dream
And join the passengers, who seem
To be unaware
Of my presence there—
Bleak eyes stare
At moon's beam.

The silence grows, as does the chill.
Then night songs of a whippoorwill
Disable the spell.
The travelers tell
What befell
And falls still:

"A brother died at Chancellorsville.
Flames razed the homes atop the hill.
Below Marye's Height
Men moaned through the night,
Maimed despite
Surgeon's skill."

Enraged, I roar that one must pay.
"Who bears the blame, the Blue or Gray?"
But the riders glare
And whisper, "Beware!
Cannons flare;
Soldiers slay."

We reach the graveyard; the horse slows.
St. George's stained glass window glows.
Thick fog swirls around.
They pass without sound.
On the ground
Lies a rose.

~Fredericksburg, Virginia

The Tryst

(A *Clogyrnach*)

A spirit wanders Chatham's Height
On slippered feet that neither light
Nor linger when her
Shrouded passions stir.
June thunder
Rends the night

That cloaks her journey to the dock.
When lightning forks, her wedding frock
Illumines the slope
And plans to elope:
Laddered rope
Thwarted lock.

In life she loved beneath her sphere,
But servants held her honor dear,
And she was betrayed.
Her vows were unmade—
Love was laid
To rest here.

With bitter heart and broken will,
She sailed, distraught, for London's chill.
At death she defied
The knots honor tied.
Dressed as bride,
She walks still.

~Chatham Manor, Fredericksburg, Virginia

Thunder Lizards

(A *Cyhydedd Hir*)

Winter solstice burns
Rocks among the ferns.
Canny eye discerns
A print unknown.

As the day unseams,
Reptiles rove my dreams;
Olden jungle teems
With beasts that hone

Tooth and claw on fright.
Sunset slants the light;
Phantoms fade from sight.
In search of bone,

Children run unshod,
Armed with goldenrod—
Thunder lizards trod
Upon this stone.

~Gari Melchers' Belmont, Fredericksburg, Virginia

Grace

(A *Rannaigheacht Ghairid*)

Hands of grace
Brushed the brow of hardship's face,
Held the heart without a home,
Spaded loam, and spurned white lace.

Bloemendaal
Holds her magic in its hall.
Dim lights dance and doors unclose;
Scent of rose where faint steps fall

Leaves a trace:
Young hearts find her hiding place
When they wander glamoured ground
Flower-crowned by hands of grace.

~Bloemendaal House, Lewis Ginter Botanical Garden,
   Richmond, Virginia

Longing

(A *Rannaigheacht Ghairid*)

Beds of moss
Beckon me to step across
Threshold of a magic realm
Gates of elm enframe the fosse.[3]

Whispers call
Wary ones to waterfall
Curtained by the spruce and fir:
"Wander through the verdant hall,

Leave your loss,
Skim the sweetness from the dross."
Maidenhair[4] entangles dreams,
Binds the seams to beds of moss.

~Maymont Gardens, Richmond, Virginia

---

[3] A ditch or moat
[4] A fern known for its delicate fronds

The Weather Vane

(A *Rhupunt*)

A longing calls
Through slumber's halls—
I leap the walls
That hold the tide

Of jeweled night.
My hooves alight
On heaven's height.
With none astride,

I navigate
The stars of fate
And seek the gate
To hopes denied.

Though doubts profane
The dark domain
Where love has lain,
Daydreams abide.

~Birthplace of Secretariat at the Meadow,
  Doswell, Virginia

The Cherokee Wedding

(A *Rannaigheacht Ghairid*)

Evenfall—
Priestess dons the sacred shawl.
In these hills where cougars prowl,
Great horned owl with haunting call

Guards the place
Where the remnants of a race
Dance in secret by the lake.
Shakers of the carapace

Move with grace
To the singer's rhythmic bass
And the beat of water drums.
Priestess comes with wedding vase.

Rite is done.
Gifts of corn and venison
Seal sacred vows of lovers—
Blanket covers two as one.

Two untwine—
Cedar, holly, spruce, and pine,
Sacred evergreens surround
Clans bound where no walls confine.

Night birds call—
Shoulder longings, soar with all,
Kindle stars with sparks of dreams
On moonbeams at evenfall.

~Cherokee, North Carolina

Once

(A *Rhupunt*)

A peacock struts
Through weeds and ruts
Where field abuts
An old estate

On weary land.
The foyer and
The stairs, once grand,
Have sagged with weight

Of barren years.
Dark dust adheres
To chandeliers
Of tarnished plate.

Once home, once inn,
Now willed to kin
Who've never been
Beyond the gate,

This manse decays.
The keeper grays,
And yet she stays
To tend the grate

At evenfall.
An eerie call
Dissolves the pall;
Cries resonate

When daylight dies.
Bejeweled eyes
Fan sun-burned skies
And undulate

With stately pace.
Rich plumes begrace,
Enchant this place—
Once more ornate.

~Bon Haven, Spartanburg, South Carolina

After the Day

(A *Clogyrnach*)

Dusk dims the light and veils this farm's
Forgotten face and homespun charms.
Behind rusted gates
A crow cultivates
Earth that waits
For tanned arms

To harness moody mules to plow.
No wrinkled face with sweaty brow
Lifts toward welcome rain.
Equine weather vane
Tosses mane,
Jumps a bough,

And pivots toward the Pleiades
Before an unseen hand can seize
The reins or halter.
Tarnished hooves falter:
Tracks alter
With the breeze.

Then moonlight cools July's hard heat
And silvers errant stalks of wheat.
With darkness erased
My memories taste
Of dreams chased—
Bittersweet.

~The Old Homestead, Jeffersonville, Georgia

Border Walls

(A *Rannaigheacht Ghairid*)

Stone by stone,
Hardened hands clear fields unsown;
Weary arms fell long-leaf pine—
Rocks define the land we own.

Dry-stack walls
Rise as our ambition sprawls
Through a mansion with locked gates—
Worth equates with gilded halls.

Marble hearts
Do not bleed when pricked by darts,
But our turrets block the light.
From this night, no one departs:

Unbeknown,
We have buried flesh with bone
And entombed our children here—
Vaults of fear rise stone by stone.

~Homewood, Asheville, North Carolina

Polar Night

(A *Rannaigheacht Ghairid*)

Robed in white,
Specters dance with northern light.
Lumbering with silent gait,
A great ice bear haunts the night.

Ghostly growls
Ride the air with snowy owls.
Shamans say she swam the sound—
Her cubs drowned; her spirit prowls.

Melted floes—
Weariness and hunger's throes
Clawed her offspring from her paws.
Her jaws snapped at faceless foes.

Black of night—
No ice glows in Arctic light.
No titans roam this dark and
Lonely land, bereft of white.

~Fairbanks, Alaska

Hunters

(A *Clogyrnach*)

The sun has fired his forge today
And dipped his tongs in Glacier Bay.
Warm waters plunder,
Ice cracks asunder,
Calves thunder,
Break away,

And drift past hungry polar bears
That lumber far from frozen lairs.
Until the ice heals
No air hole reveals
That ringed seals
Climb the stairs

To venture from their frigid cell
Where bones of ships and sailors dwell.
The ice bears grow thin—
No flipper or fin
Breaks the skin
Of this well.

A starving bear swims to a floe
While cubs sleep in the depths below.
Orion grants grace,
Sights the sun, gives chase,
Strikes day's face
With his bow.

Polaris will not rise tonight
For blizzards pluck the stars from sight.
An angry wind howls
With echoes of growls.
Darkness cowls
The moonlight.

~Glacier Bay, Alaska

Northern Lights

(A *Clogyrnach*)

Worn totems stare with sightless eyes
Through depths of dreams where faint moon lies.
She hums her death hymn
And soft light grows dim—
Silver rim
Cannot rise.

Her face is scorched by summer's blaze
As sleepless sun turns nights to days.
Voracious, he feeds
And darkness recedes.
Glacier bleeds,
Ice decays.

When fireweed paints the valleys red
The ice bear hungers; seals have fled.
His fangs drip with growls;
Wolves answer with howls.
Wood wraith prowls
For undead.

A snowy owl on silent wings
Bears magic gifts from Arctic kings.
A cloak of black thread
Enchants the sun's bed.
Spells are said—
Night shade sings.

~Fairbanks, Alaska

At Standing Rock

(A *Rhupunt*)

The serpent comes.
Its black blood hums
As venom numbs
The lakes and land.

No treaties hold.
The white men sold
Their word for gold
Before they manned

The hungry drill
That pierced Black Hill.
Soon oil will fill
The veins law banned.

They tunneled deep—
Black bile will seep
Where old bones sleep
In sacred sand.

At death, at birth,
Red feet kiss earth.
Her life is worth
The flames we fanned

At Standing Rock.
Our bodies block
The fangs that lock
On Mother's hand.

Our home we hold
Despite the cold.
We will not fold
On rocks that stand.

~Standing Rock Sioux Reservation, North Dakota

Gemstones of the Desert

(A *Rannaigheacht Ghairid*)

Sun-fired stone
Frames a shattered bison bone
Pinned to earth by ancient lance.
Diamonds dance their warning tone.

Slumber's shores—
Glittering eyes close their doors.
On cloudless sea, heat waves crest—
Ringtails rest in cactus cores.

Breathless, still—
No breeze stirs the dust until
Burned-out sun slides into bed,
Bleeding, red, in twilight's chill.

Tongues unknown
Call the moon to hold the throne.
Though men search for gems to steal,
Shades conceal the sun-fired stone.

~Phoenix, Arizona

Sedona

(A *Rhupunt*)

Deep shadows fade
Red rock cascade
To purpled jade—
Sun sparks ignite.

Stone sentries stare
Sightless through air
At treadless stair
Spanning the height.

No mortals dare
Enter the lair
Or linger where
Spirit meets sprite.

This shrine of stone
And bleached white bone
Hides secrets shown
In the moonlight.

~Sedona, Arizona

The Garden of the Gods

(A *Cywydd Llosgyrnog*)

When storm clouds hid the Manitou[5],
They cloaked invaders from his view:
Giants who engendered fright

With fearsome height and thundered tread.
Their horrid creatures ran ahead—
Kindled dread and panicked flight.

Before their jaws devoured the land,
A shaman knelt upon the sand,
Raised a hand toward sacred height—

He chanted prayers and pleas for grace,
Implored the God to show His face,
And unbrace the giants' might.

The clouds dispersed; the Spirit spoke.
The hostile race stood still as oak,
Scorched by smoke that shuttered sight

And burned their bodies into stone.
The wind now whittles flesh from bone,
Carves a throne where kestrels light.

---

[5] An Algonquian term for a spiritual force that controls nature

As vestiges of day unseam
Within the vortex of a dream,
Weathergleam[6] forestalls the night.

~The Garden of the Gods, Colorado Springs, Colorado

---

[6] Light or clear sky at the horizon

Sacred Songs

(A *Rhupunt*)

When earth is young
Secrets are sung
In Tiwa[7] tongue—
The shaman's prose.

As starlight spills
Day's hot breath chills.
White stags roam hills
Where sagebrush grows.

Dim firelight falls
On earthen walls,
Crones clutch their shawls.
The deer dance slows

To steady beat
Of hearts and feet
Where spirits meet
On high plateaus.

While young men feast
The kiva[8] priest
Turns bleak eyes east—
In dreams foreknows

---

[7] Language of the Taos Pueblo tribe
[8] A large chamber used for religious rituals of the Pueblo people

That piñon smoke
Will fell the oak;
Brave blood will soak
The hands of foes.

Pale men will kill
And maim until
The plains lie still,
Red arms rest bows,

And limbs grow cold.
For God, for gold,
For tales untold,
The white death crows.

But dead will rise
For loved one's eyes
At fall moonrise
Where cascade flows.

To thwart the thief
Of souls, the chief
Leads those in grief
Where magic glows

And streams run deep.
Three white stags leap
Ahead, up steep
Paths no one knows.

Blood mountains quake.
Beneath Blue Lake
Cloud spirits wake
From long repose.

When daylight comes
El Salto hums
To pulse of drums.
Thin places close.

~Taos, New Mexico

Spires

(A *Rannaigheacht Ghairid*)

Redwoods wait—
Sentinels with spears held straight
Guard the realm where night meets day,
Stay the sun at sylvan gate.

Dusk abides
Where the spotted owlet glides.
In this forested cocoon
Moon no longer leads the tides,

And time slows.
Doors to decades past unclose—
Echoes of a Miwok drum
Summon shamans from death's doze.

Lofty spires
Lift Orion when he tires.
Fingers brush a sacred face,
Grip the grace of diamond fires.

Linger late!
Look with awe and meditate
On the bridge from earth to sky.
Rungs are high, but redwoods wait.

~Muir Woods National Monument,
  Mill Valley, California

Afterword

The Power of Bardic Verse

I wish to thank you, the reader, for joining me on this journey to places that have spoken to my heart. Some of the sites are well known, but others lie at the end of quiet roads devoid of tourists. However, all of the places that ground the pages of this book have much to tell, for human triumphs and tragedies have woven themselves into the fabric of these landscapes. As I walked along paths that carry the weight of so much history, perhaps threads of long-forgotten stories tugged at the corners of my subconscious mind. Perhaps timeless tunes on fiddles called for the company of words. To give voice to the unspoken, it seemed most fitting to draw upon the structured rhythms of bardic verse that have conveyed the collective memory of the people of Britain for centuries.

In Celtic tradition, the bard held a place of honor, and his work was often considered magical as well as prophetic. It is my fervent hope that each of the poems in this volume has captured that magic of another place, another time, and another perspective. Whispers from the past may be faint, but sometimes a receptive heart can hear the language of bones.

Notes

Bardic Verse Forms
The British Isles are home to two major classes of bardic verse: Welsh and Gaelic. In the fourteenth century the Welsh poetic forms were codified into twenty-four official meters. This collection includes four such forms: the *cywydd llosgyrnog,* the *rhupunt,* the *clogyrnach,* and the *cyhydedd hir.* The Gaelic forms have not been codified in an official manner, but more than two dozen have survived. In this volume, the Gaelic forms are represented by the *rannaigheacht ghairid.*

"Jane"
In 2012 archaeologists discovered the mutilated skeleton of a young girl in the debris of a James Fort cellar. Since there are no records of her identity, researchers named her "Jane." Her remains provided physical evidence that Jamestown colonists resorted to cannibalism during the winter of 1609-1610, which they termed the "starving time."

The Virginia Company of London recruited labor for the Jamestown colony by providing passage to emigrants who signed indentured servitude contracts.

The water moccasin is a venomous semi-aquatic snake found in the southeastern United States.

"Trail of Tears"
The discovery of gold in Dahlonega, Georgia, generated a flood of prospectors eager to mine the land populated by the Cherokee. The United States Army forcibly removed the Cherokee Nation from its ancestral territory over the years 1838-1839. According to some estimates, approximately 4000 of the 16,000 Cherokee died on the westward march they call the "Trail of Tears."

Fairy stones are staurolite crystals that form a distinctive cross.

"Chatham Manor"
Chatham Manor, a stately home that overlooks the town of Fredericksburg, Virginia, served as a hospital for Union troops in 1862 during the Battle of Fredericksburg of the American Civil War.

"Traveller"
Traveller, General Robert E. Lee's favorite war horse, was an iron-gray Saddlebred that survived the American Civil War and outlived his master. Traveller's bones are buried outside the Lee family crypt on the campus of Washington and Lee University. His stable still stands, and tradition requires that the door be left open so the horse's spirit can wander freely.

Curry combs are hand-held tools with serrated teeth that are used to groom horses.

"Angels of Marye's Heights"
In the Battle of Fredericksburg, approximately 8000 Union troops fell in a futile attempt to dislodge Confederate forces entrenched on Marye's Heights. During the night of 13 December 1862, hundreds of wounded Union men remained trapped in the exposed area beneath the stone wall that bordered the "Sunken Road." Legend holds that Sergeant Richard Kirkland, a nineteen-year-old Confederate soldier, was so moved by their plaintive cries that the next day he left the shelter of the wall to provide them with water. Thereafter he was known as "the Angel of Marye's Heights."

"Holy Grail"
Saint Francis of Assisi is known as the patron saint of animals.

In 1862 Union troops occupied parts of Stafford County opposite Fredericksburg, Virginia. That spring and summer, approximately 10,000 slaves crossed the Rappahannock River to pass through Union lines to freedom.

"Restitution"
In May 1863 the Confederate Army of Northern Virginia defeated the Union Army of the Potomac at Chancellorsville, Virginia. This victory proved costly for the South in that it claimed the life of Lieutenant General Stonewall Jackson. In the darkness of May 2, Jackson's men fired on him by mistake. The wounds inflicted cost him an arm, and eight days later he succumbed to complications.

On December 11-15, 1862, Union forces battled Confederate troops for control of Fredericksburg. Combatants numbering just under 200,000 clashed in the streets of this riverside town and the surrounding areas. The Union army was unable to dislodge Confederate soldiers entrenched on Marye's Heights and withdrew after sustaining heavy losses.

"The Tryst"
Local legend holds that when he was a guest at Chatham Manor, George Washington intercepted a young lady in the act of eloping with a drysalter. Her father, who expected an alliance with someone of higher social standing, forced her to return to England, where a more suitable marriage could be arranged. The heartbroken "Lady in White" supposedly walks the grounds of Chatham every seven years on the anniversary of her death.

"Thunder Lizards"
Although no dinosaur bones have been found in Virginia, several areas have footprint-bearing rocks. Dr. Robert E. Weems has identified footprints of six types of dinosaurs in the stones installed as pathways at Belmont Estate in Fredericksburg.

"Grace"
The social reformer Grace Arents converted her estate, Bloemendaal, into a convalescent home for children and then a model farm. This unassuming heiress pursued gardening with a passion, and her experimental agricultural techniques attracted many visitors to "Flower Valley." She avoided publicity and cameras, but one telling photograph shows her dressed in pants and seated cross-legged on the ground. Upon her death in 1926, she bequeathed the property to the city of Richmond as a botanical garden and public park in honor of her beloved uncle, Lewis Ginter. Her mischievous spirit is said to wander Bloemendaal House, and "Miss Grace" is supposedly at work when lights flicker and doors close mysteriously.

"Longing"
In 1886 James Henry and Sallie May Dooley purchased farmland along the James River and began the process of creating Maymont, an estate that captured the grandeur of America's Gilded Age. Having no children, the couple bequeathed the mansion and grounds to the city of Richmond.

The Japanese Garden at Maymont features a large waterfall and a woodland path that skirts the pond. In accordance with Eastern landscaping principles, earth tones predominate. Strategically planted water iris, water lilies, and cherry trees provide contrasting color.

"The Weather Vane"
In 1973 Secretariat astounded horse racing fans by crossing the finish line at the Belmont Stakes thirty-one lengths ahead of his closest challenger. With this victory the Thoroughbred affectionately known as "Big Red" established a new world record, secured the Triple Crown, and earned a reputation as one of the greatest race horses of all time. His birthplace at the Meadow in Doswell has been listed on the National Register of Historic Places and the Virginia Landmarks Register.

"The Cherokee Wedding"
The United States Army forcibly removed the Cherokee Nation from its ancestral territory during the years 1838-1839, but some members of the tribe escaped and fled to the foothills of the Blue Ridge Mountains in North Carolina.

Cherokee ceremonial rattles are often constructed from turtle shells. During a traditional Cherokee wedding, the man and woman share a single drinking vessel with two openings.

"Once"
Bon Haven, a historic brick mansion in Spartanburg, South Carolina, has been unoccupied since 1995. The main house was built in the French Second Empire style in 1884. Subsequent additions included Neoclassical columns and a portico. The estate, which originally included ninety-one acres, now spans a mere six acres. Extensive structural damage and prohibitive restoration costs have impeded efforts to salvage this abandoned home. A demolition permit was issued in February 2017, but preservationists have continued to search for a way to save the unique landmark from destruction.

"After the Day"
Like many aged wooden farmhouses in the vicinity of Middle Georgia, the Old Homestead was abandoned and left to deteriorate. The family moved into a brick house on the property.

"Border Walls"
Homewood is a stone manor in Asheville, North Carolina, that was built in 1927 as the private residence of Dr. Robert S. Carole and his wife Grace Potter Carole. Subsequent additions to the main house included a 1500-square-foot piano room and a stone turret. The couple hosted a number of private piano concerts in their home. When the composer Bela Bartok performed there, F. Scott and Zelda Fitzgerald and the Vanderbilts were among the guests. Homewood is now an event and conference center.

"Polar Night"
As the mass of sea ice in the Arctic decreases, polar bears must swim longer distances to cross open sea. Consequently, the risk of drowning is increasing, particularly for bears less than one year old. Although adult polar bears can swim for hours, their cubs do not have the strength to survive in seas devoid of ice floes.

"Hunters"
A polar bear hunts seals by lying in wait at the breathing holes they have carved in sea ice. Since polar bears cannot successfully stalk their prey in open water, they must fast when the sea is unfrozen. As rising global temperatures lengthen the periods during which feeding grounds remain ice free, the risk of starvation increases.

Chunks of ice break off the end of a glacier and produce icebergs in a process known as "calving."

According to Greek mythology, the giant hunter Orion was placed among the stars after his death. The constellation that bears his name can be seen chasing the Pleiades.

"Northern Lights"
In Fairbanks, Alaska, daylight lasts almost twenty-two hours in midsummer. Regions farther north have twenty-four hours of daylight.

Polar bears, also known as ice bears, require frozen terrain for successful hunts. When seas are free of ice, the bears cannot approach their prey undetected.

"At Standing Rock"
The Fort Laramie Treaty of 1851 recognized the sovereignty of the Lakota Sioux over the Great Plains "as long as the river flows and the eagle flies." The Fort Laramie Treaty of 1868 prohibited white settlement in the Black Hills for all time, but the subsequent discovery of gold generated an influx of miners who violated the treaty with impunity.

The Lakota protested construction of the Dakota Access Pipeline on the grounds that the project would contaminate their sole source of drinking water and disrupt their sacred lands. The completed pipeline passes under the Missouri River less than one mile upstream of the Standing Rock Reservation.

"Gemstones of the Desert"
The Western diamondback rattlesnake is a pit viper found in the Southwestern United States.

Ringtails are nocturnal mammals related to raccoons and coati. They nest in hollows of trees or other available cavities.

"Sedona"
Sedona is a desert town famous for its red sandstone formations. At sunset the rock glows in vibrant reds and oranges. Native Americans consider this area sacred, and many travelers seek spiritual enlightenment at its supposed "vortex sites," places where the earth's energy is particularly strong.

"The Garden of the Gods"
According to Native American legends, the massive rock formations of "the Garden of the Gods" are the remains of giants and their terrible beasts. When these beings threatened to devour the earth, the Chosen Ones prayed to the Manitou, who turned the invaders to stone.

"Sacred Songs"
The Sangre de Cristo (Blood of Christ) Mountains are located in southern Colorado and northern New Mexico.

Blue Lake is the most sacred shrine of the Taos Pueblo tribe. El Salto is a peak in the Taos Mountain Range that reportedly "sings" or "hums." Scientists have been unable to locate the source of the sounds.

Ancient Celts believed that the veil between the physical and spiritual worlds was more transparent in specific geographic locations known as "thin places."

"Spires"
Many of the redwoods in Muir Woods exceed 200 feet in height and are 500 to 800 years old. These massive trees filter the sunlight so that much of the forest floor is perpetually shaded.

The Miwok were Native Americans who inhabited northern California.

Acknowledgments

I am deeply grateful to the journals and anthologies that previously published some of the poems in this collection.

"Longing" and "The Weather Vane" first appeared in *Glass: Facets of Poetry*.

"After the Day" first appeared in the *Lyric*.

"Border Walls" was first published in *Quarterday: A Journal of Classical Poetry*.

"Sedona" was first published in the *Society of Classical Poets Journal;* "Polar Night," "The Garden of the Gods," and "Gemstones of the Desert" were featured on the society's web page.

"Restitution" was first published in the *Fredericksburg Literary and Art Review*.

"Once" was first published in *Mezzo Cammin*.

"Trail of Tears," "Angels of Marye's Heights," "The Cherokee Wedding," and "Holy Grail" were first published in *River Tides*.

"At Standing Rock" first appeared in *America, We Call Your Name: Poems of Resistance and Resilience*.

About the Author

Elizabeth Spencer Spragins is a writer, poet, and editor who taught in North Carolina community colleges for more than a decade before returning to her home state of Virginia. Her tanka and bardic verse in the Celtic style have been published in Europe, Asia, and North America.